I0453526

Dracopis Press

OR_ELSE_b

Small press,
or else

Kristian Carlsson

www.dracopis.com
beard@dracopis.com

Dracopis_003   OR_ELSE_b
Kristian Carlsson: Small press, or else

ISBN 978-91-87341-03-8
EUROPE. First edition.

[Also available in the USA:
ISBN 978-91-87341-05-2]

0.

Beginnings

Why should you start a small press?

No one knows better than you what good fiction is supposed to be.

No one knows better than you what is wrong with an almost picture perfect fiction.

You understand why you don't understand the major publishing houses.

You understand why you don't understand mainstream stream of consciousness.

Where should the core of this small press be constituted?

In the manifold heart of yours, by your indigestible bed, in your dreamy wardrobe. In your kitchen. In your language, in your deceitful sense of tragedy. In the very heart of your brainy mind.

Who are you, this you of you?

No, not the mad one, and never greedy. You don't have the desperation of despair. You have an urge to bring life to the diversity of the normative. You care for the alphabet and take care of the letters. No gambler, not calculative. You rescue each letter from the equations.

In order to publish a good book you must loathe bad literature.

Never rest in your present ability to make the distinguishment.

Preferably you should only read small press literature. To hell with establishment. Why else going into business? Read it not to know what readers might like, but to embrace what literature can be like.

Treat the book as a mere body, but its contents as a human mind.

Someday you'll be able to make a dream piece of literature into a dream book volume. Live by that ambition. Work your way there one book at a time letting no book be overshadowed by that ambition.

I.

Continuation

Start out small. Continue smaller if needed. Never end.

Dream big. Continue dreaming bigger if needed. Make sure to keep being considered small.

A small press is another world. One of possibilities. That is where your dreams and reality come to their common literary senses. There's no limit to a small press. As yours.

Don't hesitate about disproportionate publishing sprees. You are a small press—seven titles one year and two the next, for instance, would be a sign of qualitative willpower. Even stop publishing for a year or two, no shame in that; you shouldn't feel dictated on such an occasion to be finalizing the terminal end operation of your press.

Appreciate the difference between high expectations and high ambition. It will help you single out financial priorities.

And yes, you need to figure out basic accounting principles, at least. Even if you have someone else doing the bookkeeping. It is a crucial part of getting acquainted with and comfortable in your publishing house.

Money is always an issue—as it is powerful enough to cause divorces and wars in the world, you should be confident it might tear you and your press apart if either you or your press is not cautious enough.

If a writer can be on the brink of bankruptcy, why shouldn't a publisher?

If your small press is living on that edge, don't conceal it to your authors: Keep promises and agreements at all times—but if you can't, you shouldn't dishonor the deal-breaks with silence. Be frank. And make sure to have a limited amount of promises made at any given time. Be realistic, but not diffuse. If you can't make a promise, make something else, less binding, as long as the premises are clear.

Don't whine about economics other than to friends and family. The small press does exist for other reasons than financial. Put out books, as expected of you.

No need to explain everything you can't offer an author. Resist handing out truisms. Focus on what you do provide. But when it comes to agreeing on a percentage on book sales, which might look fancy, let it be clear that most probably it is based on next to nothing.

Be sure to know how all things in the process are done. Even if in the end you have others to do this and that. Figure out how you want things to be processed. Follow that line. Put trust in the competence of others, all the while that direction of yours is not to be broken.

If you can't educate yourself on everything, get a clear image of the possible results and expectations for each part of the process, to know what to expect of others.

Don't spend time on schools and courses. Trial and error. Throw yourself into your first project, not letting go of it until you find its outcome impeccable. Further along, however, you'll find that first book to be flawed. Otherwise you might not have understood the trial and error part and ought to go back to step one again for your unprecedented evolvement.

The small publisher always works against time. However prepared. It is to be expected. Every little step on the way amounts to a certain measure of time. And the continuous time consumption eternally accumulates somehow for each project you have ever taken on; even still by the projects you soon have forgotten—while you might be thinking there is time to save when you get to know the craftsmanship... Instead you begin making more well-reasoned decisions, finding innovative newnesses, considering obscure details. And there is the administration, the consequential butterfly effect, the correspondence, aaaarrgh... Spend time on your writers. Save time on everything else. Try at least.

If you can't manage to handle the individualities of writers as beings, don't—no don't—ever settle publishing the authors you in fact are able to connect with.

The unreasonable and unlevelled ambience of disharmony, settled between you and the author, should also—somewhat objectively—be expected to be found between the author and the literary piece. Otherwise the author hasn't done the best of ability. You would want that disharmonious tension, in the end, to cement itself between the book and the reader. Whereby the book will surely come alive. Trust your judgment on this. At every instant there should be exceptions and limitations to a tolerable disharmony. It ought to be put in perspective to what is credible—not what is endurable—to you in terms of being a publisher, an editor, a reader.

Play it safe in publishing, not in literary content. It distinguishes you from major publishers, who are doing it the other way around. Publishing a book counts for something, publishing valid literature counts for everything. Don't dismiss a good book from a major publisher, but pay no attention to it; you, as the small press.

When a book is being published, there should be no turning back. But you'll find that often there is. Set certain standards for your small press. A book ignored by its reader is ignorance. A book ignored by its publisher becomes a menace to literature.

Publish a book. And go with the flow. That publication will take you somewhere. And the book itself will take you another place. Be attentive of the flow. Next thing you know, another book is due to be published out of paths you could never predict. It's all a matter of time. Such flows are insatiable.

Publish a book—and conquer the world. You are, after all, dealing with fiction. In some proportion you'll carry it off. And at least the author will put faith in you.

2.

Maintenance

Don't be ignorant to other justified small presses.
Even those you'll never agree with.
No matter if they are miles and miles away.

Get to know what the good presses are up to.
Let them know what you have in prospect.

Sharing something saves time in many ways.

Never use war terminology as metaphor in your correspondence. You are dealing with art.

Don't repeat yourself. Even after a success.

Don't believe there is a recipe for success.
If other presses have made something prosper-ous—let them have their recipes to themselves, that is, what could be mistaken for a recipe. Even if they can repeat that success.

Reevaluate your dedication to your small press at close intervals. You are the only one who needs to be motivated.

Build a trust between publishers alike. Be trust-worthy.

Don't make use of messengers, such as the writers, even in the smallest issue.

You are in charge of maintaining the control of your brand, you are to blame whenever-whatsoever, you have the blueprint; you are the blueprint of your press. So let it be known.

By creating a well-based network of small press publishers you'll get up to date, and in touch with reality, regarding a well-balanced print run, currently favorable printers, small press book fairs worth the time, meaningful distributors and other intermediary sources for literature, dedicated book stores, et cetera.

Any small press ought to be built on the life's works of writers. But never through them.

Be sure to professionally separate the writers from your press. Tend towards the shallow namedropping of their names for marketing the depth of your press. Not the other way around.

Never steal a writer. But borrow openly.

Guard the threshold of originality in a text as property. Not the author behind it.

If an author, repetitive in writings and rejected, turns to another publisher—guard the threshold of originality only on basis of your publications. Usually no one is to blame.

Your writers won't have any reasonable earnings from being published at the small press. They stick to you for other reasons. As an additional service you could also invest time in getting your authors into public readings and mediatingly assure that their presence in the programs of others will be awarded with ready money. You can push for compensation more firmly than they would on their own behalf. Unprestigious no-pay reading offers can, in many cases, be turned at least a little more prosperous by the mediation of the publisher. Allow for such inquiries about public appearances through your small press.

3.

Reading scripts

Although unsolicited scripts might be submitted at high rate, do not count on more than one in a thousand to fit your standards.

You can only be a publishing house of your own set standard by pursuing the manuscripts to publish. That process works by networking. And you will get ahead in that by following the directions of the previous chapter in this volume.

For the sake of quality go beyond the name of the author. Albeit a name can sell the book, be sure to remember that such a book will not sell the brand of your small press; other than by gathering more unsolicited scripts for you. It happens that fresh publishers get star-struck; on a daily basis, one might suspect. Don't sell yourself short. Let your publishing house be profiled by literature, not authors.

Never dismiss something you haven't read. Also never spend time on rereading something you already dismissed, no matter what changes are being made to convince you otherwise. Unless you have directed the changes. Handle this balancing act most carefully when it comes to authors you've already published. But don't waste more time even on their bad ideas.

Be a mentor to your authors in all of your ability. They should know what you like and why you like it. They should know by heart when it would be of no use to come to you. They should be certain of your abilities.

As a small press you should unconsciously aim for your authors to leave you when they are ready to find new collaborators. That is not a loss to you. It gives you time to take on other projects. No matter if you as an editor have been a part in shaping their authorship, don't go bitter on fantasies of others now profiting by your mentorship. You have done your part. You were the mentor all along. Your small press goes way beyond any author.

Be a mentor to aspiring small press publishers as well, but don't make this ridiculously time consuming.

Never advise authors to send their manuscripts to this or that other small press instead of you taking it on. In such a rare case of knowing what is best for another press, it should be you yourself who—leaving the author unaware—mediates and allows for the other press to decide whether to contact the author.

Don't take pride in reading manuscripts in due time, read them when you can find the time. Always count on manuscripts to be at several publishers at once. If the manuscript is good and another press took it on before you could, then rejoice in it becoming a book after all. Continue reading new manuscripts when you can find the time.

Let it be known that you read manuscripts only in order of submittance. Never disclose to an inquisitive author how many are ahead in line. Stick to the non-committing timeline which is the only one you ever will be capable of withholding.

But when it comes to your reading of manuscripts, don't follow any directions, even if you made them up yourself. You will be introduced to infinities of meaningless writings. And boring ones. To stay sane you'll have to use your instincts—or gut feeling—to pinpoint the submissions worth your time. However, it will show that you rarely can trust those instincts of yours either. At least it gives you a sense of being in control of the masses of words pouring down on you.

Never answer uninformed queries from aspiring authors. If they have found your email, they most certainly can find your web page. And on your web page you should let the suitable information be known. It's either an ignorant writer asking such questions, or one that thinks asking questions, however unnecessary, will be the fast lane into your mind. Ignore them. Those who are sincere about wanting to collaborate with you specifically, are bound to then look up the information on their own.

Scripts are to be dealt with as scripts; writers not to your liking are to be dealt with as snakes. Well, maybe not snakes, but you get the drift.

If you are going to take your time valuating unsolicited manuscripts, be sure the authors have taken their time understanding your small press, and the guidelines you have put up for submissions. Don't waste time even on a splendid manuscript, if the author can't bother to follow—or is ignorant of—what as to your sayings is explicitly expected on their behalf. It should be acceptable for an author to also break all guidelines, but then it ought to be evident to you that they are intentionally broken, and furthermore broken in a manner that comes to your liking.

Never give replies to authors on manuscripts already rejected. Let them send one email. Let them send two. Keep silent. Even stop reading their correspondence. You should not spend your mentorship on those authors. Let them get angry, let them backstab your small press in public. Don't get into that mess.

4.

Editing scripts

Respect the seriousness of the writer.
Don't hesitate to suggest any changes.
Don't be afraid to insist on changes.
Respect the potential readership.

Treat the authors as you would treat a best friend, treat their manuscripts as the deceitful backbiter you are determined to get into good manners by discipline.

Help your writer kill the darlings. Make sure the readers will find their darlings. You yourself should not be in the business of having any darlings. As an editor the text is to be treated as text—not literature—to become literature.

Be forever horrified of typos. The writer of the text won't see them, as you might not in your writings of publisher's blurbs et cetera. Don't let it be up to the author to decide on the content of the blurb, but let him or her proof read it.

Proof reading is to provide the text with a pair of clean underwear.

5.

Dealing with
Translations

Translators are no authors. Even proper authors who perform the act of translation are in that sense merely translators. Take the translators for what they are; no suggestion of slighter qualities intended. For translations take use of the best translators, never judge by authorship. Naturally there should be a sensitivity of language, but no need for individuality in tone.

Wherever you stumble upon translators, somehow put them to the test. You never know when you suddenly will need one. Profiling yourself with translated fiction you should obtain an interconnection of translators in your press. This is something rather on the idle side of being bonded; don't literally start networking.

To perfect the difficult translations of distant language groups, the embodiment of the writer might need to be evolutioned within the editor, not the translator. The editor must then take charge of the text as its author once has done.

To perfect the difficult translations of related language groups, the pitfalls of kinship must be studied by the editor with the eyes of a hardy linguist. The editor must then scrutinize the text as a critic would.

In a small press the responsibility to a foreign writer ought to have heavier proportions than to the translator. The absent author needs representation beyond reasonable doubt; a manifold representation being merged out of the translator, editor, and publisher. Oftentimes the three add up to one individual in a small press, none the less play all those separate roles fairly (just resist making a show out of it). There's nothing wrong in such combinations. The unfortunate mix is many times the author translating his or her own work.

It is easier to get a translator insulted than an author; although it doesn't add up to reason. And anyhow most of the time any kind of healthy textual interference won't cause any insuperable difficulties as long as it is characteristically in context with the esthetics of your small press. Or can be attributed to original intent.

To serenely follow through the implementation of this chapter will swallow time like you've never experienced it before. Expect the publishing pace to be gravely decimated by including other than original writings. But by all means don't kill the urge if you have it. That would in the long run lead to too much inbreeding and might hit future small presses in the back. Did the small presses of the 1950's do that to the future you? Make no mistake, this pro translations decision of yours will add expandable universes to your national language of literature.

6.

Book creation

At this stage the author becomes peripheral until it's time to release the finished product. But none the less keep the author in the loop. After the intense communication during editing, the author now might be despairing if there would be a sudden period of utter silence. Show some appreciation along the line. Share some thoughts and considerations, albeit never asking for advice or opinions. It is still the author's book, but the ball is on your side of the court.

Never cut corners on a book edition for other reasons than monetary. Always "cut the corners" yourself. Make it amazing within its own limits. Then sell it as being amazing. Because you made it that way.

Stay in touch with your feelings. Seriously. They are put to better use than instincts. You must avoid sudden whims at the end of the creation. Do this by preparing your decision-making before beginning any graphic design.

Decide if the book format should be mirrored by esthetics or cost efficiency. A few quotes from a printer can help you make a moderately well-grounded decision. Same goes for binding. Presumably a lavish book could help in catching the reader's eye. But as will be stated further on in this volume, you are not to be selling books but literature.

Learn about paper. Quality, color, structure, weight, density. The proportions in grammage between cover and inlay to have a perfect bound book feeling like a book and not a brochure. Get familiar with all kinds of bindings. Study printed books in circulation. Don't fall for old-style just because; old-style means either something expensive or something cheap looking. The same goes for peachy new trends.

Proper publisher's information is needed in the book. Copyright will be assured. Contributors mentioned. But other than that there are no necessities, as in the olden days with the bastard title page and signature marks, or where to put the publisher's information page. Just make things comprehensible and accessible. And somewhat tidy.

Study fonts. Get to know distinctive characteristics of the font characters. Never take use of a font without studying it. Read up on it. Above all study it with your bare eyes. Adjust the line length of the text to the font, and them both to the language being used, and in the end to the prosody of the writer; but first of all adjust the font size in accordance to readability.

There is more to inlay design than this, as the golden rule and widows, but while reading up on it put more trust in your own observations of actual books that you find easily readable. Treat recommendations as preferences. And if you yourself have no particular preferences it is due time to attain some.

Don't give an author the mandate to decide on cover design. But at least let the authors have their saying. Covers are the manifold face of a small press, not to be confused with covers being different faces. Your backlist should not become like a randomly rigged carnival, but rather as consequent scenery. If you could find manuscripts worthy of representing your small press, so should their covers. The author works from a different angle, trying to add the perspective of his or her collected writings. You are not bound to give in to that even if you happen to be the publisher of the same collected writings. The small press always goes way beyond a single author. There is futurity at hand, don't get stuck in the moment of a single author.

7.

Selling books

Don't sell books. Sell literature.

Don't just sell. Buy books you like from other small presses. Why should your small press expect to find a consumer's motivation in potential readers if you won't spend a dime on what *you* are literarily interested in? Let expensive books be worth the expense. Let cheap books be collectible items. What goes around comes around—old but true.

A book sold without profit also adds immaterial value to your small press. But don't hesitate to be deprecatory to merchants who would add unreasonable profit margins. Even if they get the books sold. A book sold without profit by the small press should also get into the hands of the end buyer without any profits being made along the way. Monetary and immaterial values don't mix well.

End buyers are reached one by one no matter what. End buyers are not to be confused with actual readers.

You can't be sure about readership. Face it, you will never know.

But tokens of appreciation are also expressed one by one.

A small press publisher would not take comfort in the ecstasy of a sold out arena concert. And that has nothing to do with dimensions disproportional to reality, but with disproportions in factual means of measurement. The value does not equal the mass.

Publish a book with the prospect of selling the edition in ten years. In no way be fooled by the one year lifetime of major publishers' average books. In a situation where they would destroy the remainders, it's time for you to cherish the readers to come. In a situation where they have sold as many copies as they believe time and space allows for, it's time for you to relax and contemplate that there is plenty of time and space to come. When summed up, it's not given that a small press will have fewer end buyers than major companies. Not to say actual readers.

Yes, I know—you want to sell books. But in reality you won't. You want to have your books displayed at the book seller. But it won't happen. You want to have librarians drooling over your production. But your small press is not a priority.

8.

Marketing

No marketing is also part of the marketing. Just as it is said that even bad reviews are good reviews.

You can never buy every marketing space offered. Be wise. But don't judge space by the potentiality of sold books. Whatever you buy into ought to be aiming at marketing the brand of your small press. If you want to buy yourself a way to sell books with good profits, you will get disappointed; be it advertising, book fairs, or whatever. Major publishers can spend more on marketing in a year than you'll ever spend on producing books. Stay producing your books. Let marketing find its way to you on a basis of genuine interest.

Your authors are your only means of aggressive marketing. But if you suck up to the authors they won't be your serious advertisers. If you make demands on being marketed by the authors there won't be any good advertisement. You should approach this means of marketing as an additional and unsuggestingly self-assumed service on spontaneous behalf of the author.

Your published books are marketing themselves only in the hands of strangers. You are now out of control. Trust your sense of quality.

Don't count on any additional marketing to be free. It's up to you. Even if it means conscious marketing by no marketing. Quality will make itself heard in the long run. The only question is if you will live long enough to see it come through.

9.

Final observations

As a father I wouldn't compare having a small press to raising a child. Not being a pet person though, I would most certainly put the small press work effort in the same category. But be sure your small press is expecting you to treat it as a baby. In any case the relationship will be complex.

Your friends and relations won't understand this new creature; if most of them do, and even cuddle it, you aren't pushing the boundaries enough. Don't mix your friends into the envisioned customer base. You wouldn't buy a poodle because your friends like it. You know a schnauzer will do the trick.